The Seasons

AUTUMN

Written by Stephanie Hedlund • Illustrated by Stephanie Bauer

visit us at www.abdopublishing.com

Published by Magic Wagon, a division of the ABDO Group, PO Box 398166, Minneapolis, Minnesota 55439. Copyright © 2014 by Abdo Consulting Group, Inc. International copyrights reserved in all countries. All rights reserved. No part of this book may be reproduced in any form without written permission from the publisher.

Printed in the United States of America, North Mankato, Minnesota.
052013
092013
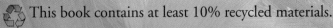 This book contains at least 10% recycled materials.

Written by Stephanie Hedlund
Illustrated by Stephanie Bauer
Edited by Rochelle Baltzer
Cover and interior layout and design by Neil Klinepier

Library of Congress Cataloging-in-Publication Data

Hedlund, Stephanie F., 1977-
  Autumn / by Stephanie Hedlund; illustrated by Stephanie Bauer.
    pages cm. -- (The seasons)
  ISBN 978-1-61641-992-9
  1. Autumn--Juvenile literature. I. Bauer, Stephanie, illustrator. II. Title.
  QB637.7.H44 2014
  508.2--dc23
                    2012049766

Contents

Autumn

There are four seasons during the year.
Do you know what season is last?
That's right, it is autumn!
Then comes winter, spring, and summer.

winter

spring

summer

Autumn

Why?

Earth travels around the sun during the year.
When Earth is tilted so the sun is over the **equator**, it is autumn.
The equator doesn't have autumn. There, the **temperatures**
stay the same for most of the year.

Equator

Earth's Axis

Day

Night

Equator

When?

The **autumnal equinox** is September 22 or 23.
On that day, the days and nights are equal all over Earth.
This is the start of autumn!

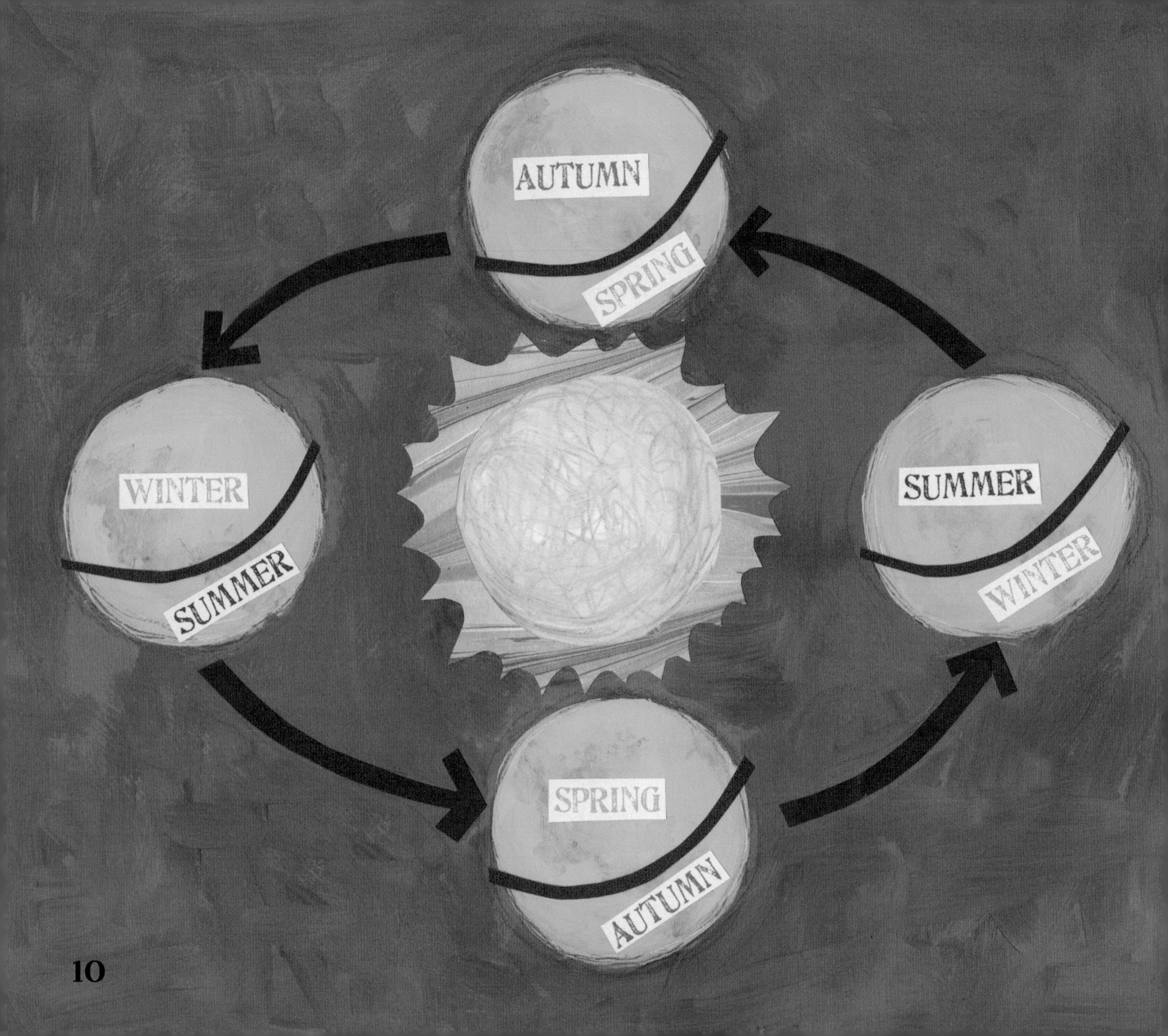
AUTUMN
SPRING
WINTER
SUMMER
SUMMER
WINTER
SPRING
AUTUMN

Autumn is also called fall.
It lasts from September to December.
Unless you live below the **equator**!
Then autumn is from March until June.

What's It Like Out?

In autumn, the **temperatures** get cooler.
The days get shorter.

When warm and cold air meet in this
season, storms can happen.
Some places have **hurricanes** in the fall.

What Do They Do?

In autumn, plants begin to go **dormant**.
Many trees lose their leaves.
Crops are ready to be **harvested**.

The animals prepare for **hibernation**.
They gather food.
Others **migrate** to warmer places.

People spend time outdoors.
They **harvest** crops and go back to school.
Soon, it will be winter!
Do you know what will happen then?

20

Seasons

January
Winter

February
Winter

March
Winter
Spring

April
Spring

May
Spring

June
Spring
Summer

Autumn Activities

Celebrate
Halloween

Go Biking

Pick
Apples

Be
Thankful

Rake
Leaves

Go Back
to School

Carve a
Pumpkin

Web Sites

To learn more about the seasons, visit ABDO Group online. Web sites about the seasons are featured on our Book Links page. These links are routinely monitored and updated to provide the most current information available.

www.abdopublishing.com

Glossary

autumnal equinox - (AH-tuhm-nahl EE-kwuh-nahks) the day in September when day and night are each twelve hours.

dormant - not active for a short time.

equator - an imaginary circle around the middle of Earth. It splits Earth into two equal parts.

harvest - what is gathered from ripe crops. A harvest may be vegetables, fruits, or grains.

hibernate - to sleep or rest during the winter months.

hurricane - a tropical storm that forms over seawater with strong winds, rain, thunder, and lightning.

migrate - to move from one place to another to find food or have babies.

temperature - (TEHM-puhr-chur) the measured level of hot or cold.

Index